The Best
Wife
in the World!

Humorous and Inspirational Quotes
Celebrating the Perfect Partner

PRION

Contents

Introduction

Being a wife is a full time job. Anyone who says otherwise is either a) your husband or b) your four-year-old child. However, unlike most rules of employment, being a wife means there is little scope for promotion or a title bump, the salary is terrible, the working hours are unbearable and, at the end of the day, there is rarely even a pat on the back for a job well done. Some days you'll dream about packing it all in and running off with the handsome courier boy, just so you don't have to unload that bloody dishwasher again. All in all, being a wife is no fun.

However, this collection of the world's funniest wife-related quotes is devoted solely to tickling the funny spots on any underappreciated wife, which last time we looked, was all of you. So, put your feet up and enjoy it.

Independent
Woman

"If I honour my needs first,
I will be the best wife, the best
mum, the best sister, the best friend.
I have to come first, because then
everyone benefits."

Gisele Bündchen

"Every man who is high up likes
to think that he has done it all
himself, and the wife smiles and
lets it go at that."

J.M. Barrie

"I don't mind living in a man's world, as long as I can be a woman in it."

Marilyn Monroe

"My mother said it was simple to keep a man. You must be a maid in the living room, a cook in the kitchen and a whore in the bedroom. I said I'd hire the other two and take care of the bedroom bit."

Jerry Hall

"Women and cats will do as they please, and men and dogs should relax and get used to the idea."

Robert A. Heinlein

"One half of the world cannot understand the pleasures of the other."

Jane Austen

"A woman needs a man like a fish needs a bicycle."

Irina Dunn

"And she's got brains enough for two, which is the exact quantity the girl who marries you will need."

P.G. Wodehouse

"People think at the end of the day that a man is the only answer to fulfillment. Actually a job is better for me."

Princess Diana

"There are no good girls gone wrong – just bad girls found out."

Mae West

"Remember, Ginger Rogers did everything Fred Astaire did, but backwards and in high heels."

Faith Whittlesey

"I never married, because
I have three pets at home that
answer the same purpose as a
husband. I have a dog that growls
every morning, a parrot that swears
all afternoon and a cat that comes
home late at night."

Marie Corelli

"I like to wake up each morning
feeling a new man."

Jean Harlow

"The thing women have yet to
learn is nobody gives you power.
You just take it."

Roseanne Barr

"A girl should be two things:
classy and fabulous."

Coco Chanel

"I'm selfish, impatient and a little insecure. I make mistakes, I am out of control and at times hard to handle. But if you can't handle me at my worst, then you sure as hell don't deserve me at my best."

Marilyn Monroe

"A liberated woman is one who has sex before marriage and a job after."

Gloria Steinem

"Men reach their sexual peak at 18.
Women reach theirs at 35.
Do you get the feeling that God is
playing a practical joke?"

Rita Rudner

"I'm tough, I'm ambitious, and
I know exactly what I want. If that
makes me a bitch, OK."

Madonna

"I do not want a husband who honours me as a queen if he does not love me as a woman."

Elizabeth I

"A man does what he can; a woman does what a man cannot."

Isabel Allende

"A woman simply is, but a man must become."

Camille Paglia

"A woman needs protecting like Rambo needs a bodyguard."

Jennifer Crusie

"In my sex fantasy, nobody ever loves me for my mind."

Nora Ephron

"I'm letting no man handle my bank account."

Hattie McDaniel

"No man succeeds without a good woman behind him. Wife or mother, if it is both, he is twice blessed indeed."

Godfrey Winn

"Women hope men will change after marriage but they don't; men hope women won't change but they do."

Bettina Arndt

"A man's best fortune, or his worst, is his wife."

Thomas Fuller

"I require only three things of a man. He must be handsome, ruthless and stupid."

Dorothy Parker

"There is more to sex appeal than just measurements. I don't need a bedroom to prove my womanliness. I can convey just as much sex appeal picking apples off a tree or standing in the rain."

Audrey Hepburn

"Why haven't I got a husband and children? I never met a man I could marry."

Greta Garbo

"I was a queen, and you took away my crown; a wife, and you killed my husband; a mother, and you deprived me of my children. My blood alone remains: take it, but do not make me suffer long."

Marie Antoinette

"Husbands and wives generally understand when opposition will be vain."

Jane Austen

"I think men who have a pierced ear are better prepared for marriage. They've experienced pain and bought jewellery."

Rita Rudner

"I would rather trust a woman's instinct than a man's reason."

Stanley Baldwin

"Women need to feel loved and men need to feel needed."

Rita Mae Brown

"You don't have to be anti-man to be pro-woman."

Jane Galvin Lewis

"Some of us are becoming the men we wanted to marry."

Gloria Steinem

"Bride. A woman with a fine prospect of happiness behind her."

Ambrose Bierce

"From the moment I was six I felt sexy. And let me tell you it was hell, sheer hell, waiting to do something about it."

Bette Davis

"I never knew what real happiness was until I got married. And by then it was too late."

Max Kauffmann

"The true index of a man's character is the health of his wife."

Cyril Connolly

"Marriage is a wonderful institution, but who wants to live in an institution?"

Groucho Marx

"Remember no one can make you
feel inferior without your consent."

Eleanor Roosevelt

"If you want to sacrifice the
admiration of many men for the
criticism of one, go ahead,
get married."

Katharine Hepburn

"Men aren't necessities.
They're luxuries."

Cher

"Women who seek to be equal
with men lack ambition."

Timothy Leary

"The only time a woman really
succeeds in changing a man is
when he's a baby."

Natalie Wood

LOVE ISN'T LOVE UNTIL
YOU GIVE IT AWAY, SHARE
SOME TO-DAY

"Men should strive to think much
and know little."

Democritus

"A good part – and definitely the
most fun part – of being a feminist
is about frightening men."

Julie Burchill

"A man in love is incomplete until
he is married. Then he's finished."

Zsa Zsa Gabor

"Men are more easily governed
through their vices than
through their virtues."

Napoleon Bonaparte

"I usually make up my mind about
a man in ten seconds, and I very
rarely change it."

Margaret Thatcher

"The ideal man doesn't exist.
A husband is easier to find."

Britt Ekland

"I like 'em big. And stupid.
Don't tell my husband."

Meg Cabot

"A man should be taller, older, heavier, uglier and hoarser than his wife."

E.W. Howe

"Let the wife make the husband glad to come home, and let him make her sorry to see him leave."

Martin Luther

"Work and children I could have. But the husband was just too much."

Diane von Furstenberg

"I couldn't stand that my husband was being unfaithful. I am Raquel Welch – understand?"

Raquel Welch

"The woman who can't influence
her husband to vote the way
she wants ought to be ashamed
of herself."

E.M. Forster

"I've never yet met a man who
could look after me. I don't need a
husband. What I need is a wife."

Joan Collins

"Beauty: the power by which
a woman charms a lover and
terrifies a husband."

Ambrose Bierce

"A wife should no more take her
husband's name than he should
hers. My name is my identity and
must not be lost."

Lucy Stone

"I don't sit around thinking that I'd like to have another husband; only another man would make me think that way."

Lauren Bacall

"'I am' is reportedly the shortest sentence in the English language. Could it be that 'I do' is the longest sentence?"

George Carlin

"Nobody will ever win the Battle of the Sexes. There's just too much fraternizing with the enemy."

Henry Kissinger

"Marrying a man is like buying something you've been admiring for a long time in a shop window. You may love it when you get it home, but it doesn't always go with everything else in the house."

Jean Kerr

"Why does a woman work ten years to change a man, then complain he's not the man she married?"

Barbra Streisand

"An easygoing husband is the one indispensable comfort of life."

Ouida

"In my house I'm the boss, my wife is just the decision-maker."

Woody Allen

"'Tis strange what a man may
do, and a woman yet think him
an angel."

William Makepeace Thackeray

"A successful man is one who makes
more money than his wife can
spend. A successful woman is one
who can find such a man."

Lana Turner

"Without feelings of respect,
what is there to distinguish men
from beasts?"

Confucius

"All that a husband or wife really
wants is to be pitied a little, praised
a little and appreciated a little."

Oliver Goldsmith

"When a man gives his opinion,
he's a man. When a woman gives
her opinion, she's a bitch."

Bette Davis

"Men can read maps better than
women. Because only the male mind
could conceive of one inch equaling
a hundred miles."

Roseanne Barr

The Good
Wife

"By all means, marry. If you get
a good wife, you'll become happy;
if you get a bad one, you'll become
a philosopher."

Socrates

"A good wife always forgives her
husband when she's wrong."

Milton Berle

"If I get married, I want to
be very married."

Audrey Hepburn

"Men are April when they woo,
December when they wed.
Maids are May when they are
maids, but the sky changes
when they are wives."

William Shakespeare

"The secrets of success are a
good wife and a steady job.
My wife told me."

Howard Nemerov

"It's not beauty but fine qualities,
my girl, that keep a husband."

Euripides

"Single women have a dreadful
propensity for being poor. Which
is one very strong argument in
favor of matrimony."

Jane Austen

"I'm a very committed wife.
And I should be committed, too, for
being married so many times."

Elizabeth Taylor

"There is no spectacle on
earth more appealing than that
of a beautiful woman in the act
of cooking dinner for someone
she loves."

Thomas Wolfe

"A wife is like a children's movie;
always underappreciated, and
without either, life would
be incomplete."

John Steinbeck

"Women will never be as successful as men because they have no wives to advise them."

Dick Van Dyke

"I live to succeed, not to please you or anyone else."

Marilyn Monroe

"All you need for happiness is a good gun, a good horse and a good wife."

Daniel Boone

"Every man needs two women:
a quiet homemaker and a
thrilling nymph."

Iris Murdoch

"Whilst men may play the game,
women know the score."

Habeeb Akande

"A sweetheart is a bottle of wine,
a wife is a wine bottle."

Charles Baudelaire

"What makes men indifferent to
their wives is that they can see them
when they please."

Ovid

"The woman's vision is deep
and reaching, the man's far
reaching. With the man the world
is his heart, with the woman the
heart is her world."

Betty Grable

"If you would have a good
wife, marry one who has been
a good daughter."

Thomas Fuller

"It is a truth universally
acknowledged, that a single man in
possession of a good fortune, must
be in want of a wife."

Jane Austen

"Women are meant to be loved,
not to be understood."

Oscar Wilde

"A woman's place in public is to sit beside her husband, be silent, and be sure her hat is on straight."

Bess Truman

"For a man wins nothing better than a good wife, and then again nothing deadlier than a bad one."

Hesiod

"What would men be without women? Scarce, sir... mighty scarce."

Mark Twain

"Men always want to be a woman's first love – women like to be a man's last romance."

Oscar Wilde

"I have too many fantasies to be a housewife... I guess I am a fantasy."

Marilyn Monroe

"Love your wife, your servant and your enemy equally, and file her credit card bills under the 'enemy' folder."

Bauvard

"The caterpillar does all the work, but the butterfly gets all the publicity."

George Carlin

"Heaven will be no heaven to me if I do not meet my wife there."

Andrew Jackson

"Only time can heal your broken heart. Just as only time can heal his broken arms and legs."

Jim Henson

"O my love, my wife!
Death, that hath suck'd the
honey of thy breath
Hath had no power yet upon
thy beauty."

William Shakespeare

"Happy is the man who finds a true
friend, and far happier is he who
finds that true friend in his wife."

Franz Schubert

"Some people claim that marriage interferes with romance. There's no doubt about it. Anytime you have a romance, your wife is bound to interfere."

Groucho Marx

"Many marriages would be better if the husband and the wife clearly understood that they are on the same side."

Zig Ziglar

"That is, the wife must care for what the husband cares for if he is to remain resolute."

Mother Jones

"When a girl cries, few things are more worthless than a boy."

Alexandra Bracken

"Why are women so much more interesting to men than men are to women?"

Virginia Woolf

"Every night, whisper 'peace'
in your husband's ear."

Andrei A. Gromyko

"Getting married is a lot like getting
into a tub of hot water. After you
get used to it, it ain't so hot."

Minnie Pearl

"I promise to be an excellent
husband, but give me a wife who,
like the moon, will not appear
every day in my sky."

Anton Chekhov

"I have only one real hobby –
my husband."

Florence Harding

"A husband's mother and his
wife had generally better be visitors
than inmates."

Samuel Richardson

"When we got married I told my
wife 'If you leave me, I'm going
with you.' And she never did."

James Fineous McBride

"An ideal wife is any woman who has an ideal husband."

Booth Tarkington

"I cook to inspire my husband to pay attention to me."

Sonia Rumzi

"The relationship between husband and wife should be one of closest friends."

B.R. Ambedkar

"Your wife is always right. Very simple. I think I'm going to get it tattooed on my forehead."

Hugh Jackman

"When a man steals your wife there is no better revenge than to let him keep her."

Sacha Guitry

"When you like what you like, it makes it easy for your husband to shop for you!"

Niecy Nash

"The best way to remember your wife's birthday is to forget it once."

E. Joseph Cossman

"If women are expected to do the same work as men, we must teach them the same things."

Plato

"There are only three things women need in life: food, water and compliments."

Chris Rock

"Women cannot complain about men anymore until they start getting better taste in them."

Bill Maher

"Love thy neighbour and if he happens to be tall, debonair and devastating, it will be that much easier."

Mae West

"The clog of all pleasure, the luggage of life, is the best can be said for a very good wife."

John Wilmot, 2nd Earl of Rochester

"I have learned that only two things are necessary to keep one's wife happy. First, let her think she's having her own way. And second, let her have it."

Lyndon B. Johnson

"Behind every successful man is a woman, behind her is his wife."

Groucho Marx

"I prefer the word 'homemaker' because 'housewife' always implies that there may be a wife someplace else."

Bella Abzug

"You only require two things in life: your sanity and your wife."

Tony Blair

"If you treat your wife like a thoroughbred, you'll never end up with a nag."

Zig Ziglar

"For a man wins nothing better than a good wife, and then again nothing deadlier than a bad one."

Hesiod

"A man's wife has more power over him than the state has."

Ralph Waldo Emerson

"Nothing flatters a man as much as the happiness of his wife; he is always proud of himself as the source of it."

Samuel Johnson

"There are three faithful friends –
an old wife, an old dog and
ready money."

Benjamin Franklin

"There is no such thing as being
good to your wife."

Gertrude Stein

"A man is in general better pleased when he has a good dinner upon his table, than when his wife talks Greek."

Samuel Johnson

"I fell in love with my wife 20 years ago. I am only now, it seems, getting it through my very thick skull how lucky I am."

Richard Schiff

Love and
Marriage

"Love is an ideal thing, marriage
a real thing."

Johann Wolfgang von Goethe

"Marriage: the most advanced form
of warfare in the modern world."

Malcolm Bradbury

"I love you no matter what you
do, but do you have to do so
much of it?"

Jean Illsley Clarke

"I love you and it's getting worse."

Joseph E. Morris

"Marriage is neither heaven nor
hell, it is simply purgatory."

Abraham Lincoln

"A wedding is just like a funeral
except that you get to smell
your own flowers."

Grace Hansen

"It is sometimes essential for a husband and a wife to quarrel – they get to know each other better."

Johann Wolfgang Goethe

"All marriage is such a lottery – the happiness is always an exchange – though it may be a very happy one – still the poor woman is bodily and morally the husband's slave. That always sticks in my throat."

Queen Victoria

"Marriage is a wonderful
invention: then again, so is a
bicycle repair kit."

Billy Connolly

"Marriage is an adventure,
like going to war."

G.K. Chesterton

"A marriage is always made
up of two people who are prepared
to swear that only the other
one snores."

Terry Pratchett

"All marriages are happy.
It's the living together afterward
that causes all the trouble."

Raymond Hull

"My wife was too beautiful for words, but not for arguments."

John Barrymore

"Love is hiding who you are at all times. It's wearing makeup to bed and going to Burger King to poop."

Tina Fey

"Marry a man your own age; as your beauty fades, so will his eyesight."

Phyllis Diller

"Men marry women with the hope they will never change. Women marry men with the hope they will change. Invariably they are both disappointed."

Albert Einstein

"Never take a wife till thou hast a house (and a fire) to put her in."

Benjamin Franklin

"That's what a man wants in a wife, mostly; he wants to make sure one fool tells him he's wise."

George Eliot

"Women need a reason to have sex. Men just need a place."

Billy Crystal

"One advantage of marriage is that, when you fall out of love with him or he falls out of love with you, it keeps you together until you fall in again."

Judith Viorst

"Love is a fire. But whether it is going to warm your hearth or burn down your house, you can never tell."

Joan Crawford

"Before you marry a person, you should first make them use a computer with slow Internet service to see who they really are."

Will Ferrell

"My mother once told me that if a married couple puts a penny in a pot for every time they make love in the first year, and takes a penny out every time after that, they'll never get all the pennies out of the pot."

Armistead Maupin

"Husbands are chiefly good as lovers when they are betraying their wives."

Marilyn Monroe

"Honesty is the key to a relationship. If you can fake that, you're in."

Richard Jeni

"God created sex. Priests created marriage."

Voltaire

"After seven years of marriage,
I am sure of two things: first, never
wallpaper together and second,
you'll need two bathrooms... both
for her. The rest is a mystery, but a
mystery I love to be involved in."

Dennis Miller

"A successful marriage requires
falling in love many times, always
with the same person."

Mingon McLaughlin

"I love being married. It's so great to find that one special person you want to annoy for the rest of your life."

Rita Rudner

"Love: a temporary insanity curable by marriage."

Ambrose Bierce

"It is not a lack of love, but a lack of friendship that makes unhappy marriages."

Friedrich Nietzsche

"When you're in a relationship, if you don't fight, it's not a real relationship. You have to have arguments and tensions, otherwise I don't believe it."

Richard LaGravenese

"All a girl really wants from a guy is for him to prove to her that they are not all the same."

Marilyn Monroe

"Love is being stupid together."

Paul Valery

"People stay married because they want to, not because the doors are locked."

Paul Newman

"After marriage, husband and wife become two sides of a coin; they just can't face each other, but still they stay together."

Hemant Joshi

"There are two theories to arguing with a woman. Neither works."

Will Rogers

"My wife holds the kite strings that let me go 'weeeeeee', then she reels me back in."

Jeff Bridges

"They say all marriages are made in heaven, but so are thunder and lightning."

Clint Eastwood

"Before we make love my husband takes a pain killer."

Joan Rivers

"My husband said he needed more space... so I locked him outside."

Roseanne Barr

"Coming together is a beginning; keeping together is progress; working together is success."

Henry Ford

"If love is the answer, could you please rephrase the question?"

Lily Tomlin

"The secret of a happy marriage remains a secret."

Henry Youngman

"Before marriage, a man will lie awake thinking about something you said; after marriage, he'll fall asleep before you finish saying it."

Helen Rowland

"To keep your marriage brimming,
with love in the wedding cup,
whenever you're wrong, admit it;
whenever you're right, shut up."

Ogden Nash

"The road to success is filled
with women pushing their
husbands along."

Thomas Robert Dewar

"Marriage is not kickboxing,
it's salsa dancing."

Amit Kalantri

"A dress that zips up the back will
bring a husband and wife together."

James H. Boren

"A lot of good arguments are
spoiled by some fool who knows
what he is talking about."

Miguel de Unamuno

"Like good wine, marriage gets better with age – once you learn to keep a cork in it."

Gene Perret

"The husband who wants a happy marriage should learn to keep his mouth shut and his checkbook open."

Groucho Marx

"Keep your eyes wide open before marriage, and half shut afterwards."

Benjamin Franklin

"I know what it is to live entirely for and with what I love best on earth. I hold myself supremely blest beyond what language can express; because I am my husband's life as fully as he is mine."

Charlotte Brontë

"A great marriage is not when the 'perfect couple' comes together. It is when an imperfect couple learns to enjoy their differences."

Dave Meurer

"Never get married in college; it's hard to get a start if a prospective employer finds you've already made one mistake."

Elbert Hubbard

"Marriage is give and take.
You'd better give it to her or
she'll take it anyway."

Joey Adams

"Never ruin an apology
with an excuse."

Kimberly Johnson

"In a happy marriage it is the
wife who provides the climate, the
husband the landscape."

Gerald Brenan

"I support gay marriage. I believe gay people have a right to be as miserable as the rest of us."

Kinky Friedman

"An early rising man is a good spouse but a bad husband."

Gabriel García Márquez

"There's a way of transferring funds that is even faster than electronic banking. It's called marriage."

James Holt McGavran

"Next to being married, a girl likes to be crossed in love a little now and then."

Jane Austen

"My husband and I didn't sign a prenuptial agreement. We signed a mutual suicide pact."

Roseanne Barr

"I give unto my wife my second best bed with the furniture."

William Shakespeare

"Marriage is more than finding the right person… it is being the right person!"

Elizabeth George

"Marriage is really tough because you have to deal with feelings and lawyers."

Richard Pryor

"A good marriage would be between a blind wife and a deaf husband."

Michel de Montaigne

"If any difference should be made by law between husband and wife, reason, justice and humanity, if their voices were heard, would dictate that it should be in her favour."

Ernestine Rose

"I wouldn't want to marry
anybody who was wicked, but
I think I'd like it if he could be
wicked and wouldn't."

L.M. Montgomery

"Marriage is a good deal like a
circus: there is not as much in it as
is represented in the advertising."

Edgar Watson Howe

"A happy marriage is a
long conversation which always
seems too short."

Andre Maurois

"Marriage is indeed a
manoeuvring business."

Jane Austen

"Love is a lot like a backache.
It doesn't show up on X-rays, but
you know it's there."

George Burns

"The only time a wife listens to her husband is when he's asleep."

Chuck Jones

"Marriage is like a coffin and each kid is another nail."

Homer Simpson

"The supreme art of war is to subdue the enemy without fighting."

Sun Tzu

"Marriage is the triumph of
imagination over intelligence.
Second marriage is the triumph of
hope over experience."

Oscar Wilde

"My best birth control now is just
to leave the lights on."

Joan Rivers

"Of all the home remedies,
a good wife is best."

Kin Hubbard

"In every marriage more than a week old, there are grounds for divorce. The trick is to find and continue to find grounds for marriage."

Robert Anderson

"The longest sentence you can form with two words is: I do."

H.L. Mencken

"Marriage: a book of which the first chapter is written in poetry and the remaining chapters written in prose."

Beverly Nichols

"Plant and your spouse plants with you; weed and you weed alone."

Jean Jacques Rousseau

"My parents only had one argument in 45 years. It lasted 43 years."

Cathy Ladman

"What counts in making a happy marriage is not so much how compatible you are, but how you deal with incompatibility."

Leo Tolstoy

"An archaeologist is the best husband any woman can have; the older she gets, the more interested he is in her."

Agatha Christie

"He that has not got a wife is not yet a complete man."

Benjamin Franklin

"Happy wife, happy life."

Paul Orfalea

"The problem with marriage is that it ends every night after making love, and it must be rebuilt every morning before breakfast."

Gabriel García Márquez

"A man would prefer to come home to an unmade bed and a happy woman than to a neatly made bed and an angry woman."

Marlene Dietrich

Keeping it in
the Family

"Anybody who believes that the way to a man's heart is through his stomach flunked geography."

Robert Byrne

"A happy home is one in which each spouse grants the possibility that the other may be right, though neither believes it."

Don Fraser

"Between a man and his wife
nothing ought to rule but love."

William Penn

"Can you imagine a world without
men? There'd be no crime and
lots of fat, happy women."

Nicole Hollander

"The family — that dear octopus from whose tentacles we never quite escape, nor, in our inmost hearts, ever quite wish to."

Dodie Smith

"A bachelor is a guy who never made the same mistake once."

Phyllis Diller

"The only time to eat diet food
is while you're waiting for the
steak to cook."

Julia Child

"The total amount of undesired
sex endured by women is probably
greater in marriage than in
prostitution."

Bertrand Russell

"Men marry. Women wed."

Raheel Farooq

"If you want to know about a man
you can find out an awful lot by
looking at who he married."

Kirk Douglas

"Only married people understand
you can be miserable and happy
at the same time."

Chris Rock

"The tragedy of machismo is that a man is never quite man enough."

Germaine Greer

"Obviously, if I was serious about having a relationship with someone longterm, the last people I would introduce him to would be my family."

Chelsea Handler

"If you want to look young and thin, hang around old, fat people."

Jim Eason

"A waist is a terrible thing to mind."

Tom Wilson

"Food is like sex: when you abstain, even the worst stuff begins to look good."

Beth McCollister

"One frequently only finds out
how really beautiful a women
is, until after considerable
acquaintance with her."

Mark Twain

"If you can make a woman laugh,
you can make her do anything."

Marilyn Monroe

"It is such a happiness when
good people get together –
and they always do."

Jane Austen

"Basically my wife was immature.
I'd be at home in the bath and she'd
come in and sink my boats."

Woody Allen

"There is nothing like a good dose of another woman to make a man appreciate his wife."

Clare Boothe Luce

"A woman asking 'Am I good? Am I satisfied?' is extremely selfish. The less women fuss about themselves, the less they talk to other women, the more they try to please their husbands, the happier the marriage is going to be."

Barbara Cartland

"At every party there are two kinds of people... those who want to go home and those who don't. The trouble is, they are usually married to each other."

Ann Landers

"When we lose 20 pounds... we may be losing the 20 best pounds we have! We may be losing the pounds that contain our genius, our humanity, our love and honesty."

Woody Allen

"Do you know what it means to come home at night to a woman who'll give you a little love, a little affection, a little tenderness? It means you're in the wrong house, that's what it means."

Henry Youngman

"A man likes his wife to be just clever enough to appreciate his cleverness, and just stupid enough to admire it."

Israel Zangwill

"I haven't reported my missing credit card to the police, because whoever stole it is spending less than my wife."

Ilie Nastase

"All women become like their mothers. That is their tragedy. No man does. That's his."

Oscar Wilde

"I was married by a judge. I should have asked for a jury."

Groucho Marx

"He's a fool that marries, but he's a greater that does not marry a fool; what is wit in a wife good for, but to make a man a cuckold?"

William Wycherley

"All you need is love. But a little chocolate now and then doesn't hurt."

Charles Schulz

"If ever two were one, then surely we. If ever man were loved by wife, then thee."

Anne Bradstreet

"I want a man who's kind and understanding. Is that too much to ask of a millionaire?"

Zsa Zsa Gabor

"Women are never disarmed by compliments; men always are."

Oscar Wilde

"If it can't be fixed by duct tape or WD40, it's a female problem."

Jason Love

"Marriage is a matter of give and take, but so far I haven't been able to find anybody who'll take what I have to give."

Cass Daley

"An apology? Bah! Disgusting! Cowardly! Beneath the dignity of any gentleman, however wrong he might be."

Steve Martin

"Everyone needs a house to live in, but a supportive family is what builds a home."

Anthony Liccione

"My wife said to me: 'If you won the lottery, would you still love me?' I said: 'Of course I would. I'd miss you, but I'd still love you.'"

Frank Carson

"If the family were a fruit, it would
be an orange, a circle of sections,
held together but separable – each
segment distinct."

Letty Cottin Pogrebin

"My husband and I have never
considered divorce... murder
sometimes, but never divorce."

Joyce Brothers

"Smile at each other, make time for each other in your family."

Mother Teresa

"Those who divorce aren't necessarily the most unhappy, just those neatly able to believe their misery is caused by one other person."

Alain de Botton

"If a man is talking in the forest, and there is no woman there to hear him, is he still wrong?"

Jenny Weber

"Call it a clan, call it a network, call it a tribe, call it a family: whatever you call it, whoever you are, you need one."

Jane Howard

"The old theory was 'Marry an older man, because they're more mature.' But the new theory is: 'Men don't mature. Marry a younger one.'"

Rita Rudner

"When a man opens a car door for his wife, it's either a new car or a new wife."

Prince Philip

"A woman drove me to drink and I never even had the courtesy to thank her."

W.C. Fields

"Bachelors have consciences, married men have wives."

Samuel Johnson

"Strike an average between what
a woman thinks of her husband
a month before she marries him
and what she thinks of him a year
afterward, and you will have the
truth about him."

H.L. Mencken

"Family is not an important
thing. It's everything."

Michael J. Fox

"Many a man owes his success to his first wife, and his second wife to his success."

Jim Backus

"I know why families were created with all their imperfections. They humanise you."

Anaïs Nin

"A career is wonderful, but you can't curl up with it on a cold night."

Marilyn Monroe

"If you have only one smile in
you, give it to the people you love.
Don't be surly at home, then go out
grinning at total strangers."

Maya Angelou

"Home cooking: where many a
man thinks his wife is."

Anon

The Other
Half

"Longed for him. Got him. Shit."

Margaret Atwood

"A good husband makes
a good wife."

John Florio

"If they can put one man on
the moon why can't they put
them all there?"

Chocolate Waters

"A retired husband is often a
wife's fulltime job."

Ella Harris

"Why bother with Google when
I have a wife who knows everything
about everything!"

Akshay Kumar

"One cannot be always laughing at a man without now and then stumbling on something witty."

Jane Austen

"My husband has quite simply been my strength and stay all these years, and I owe him a debt greater than he would ever claim."

Queen Elizabeth II

"A friend never defends a husband who gets his wife an electric skillet for her birthday."

Erma Bombeck

"There is a name for people who are always wrong about everything all the time... Husband!"

Bill Maher

"A good husband is never the first to go to sleep at night or the last to awake in the morning."

Honore de Balzac

"A husband is what is left of a lover, after the nerve has been extracted."

Helen Rowland

"A husband without faults is a dangerous observer."

George Savile

"Being a husband is a whole-time job. That is why so many husbands fail. They cannot give their entire attention to it."

Arnold Bennett

"A husband is very much like a house or a horse."

Anthony Trollope

"He was a dreamer, a thinker, a speculative philosopher... or, as his wife would have it, an idiot."

Douglas Adams

"A husband is like a fire − he goes out when unattended."

Evan Esar

"There is one thing more exasperating than a wife who can cook and won't, and that's a wife who can't cook and will."

Robert Frost

"Husband: a man with hopes of being a lover who settles for being a provider, causing his wife to grow suspicious of her depleting jewellery box."

Bauvard

"The husband who decides to surprise his wife is often very much surprised himself."

Voltaire

"One never realizes how different a husband and wife can be until they begin to pack for a trip."

Erma Bombeck

"Wives are people who feel they don't dance enough."

Groucho Marx

"You – poor and obscure, and small and plain as you are – I entreat to accept me as a husband."

Mr Rochester, Jane Eyre, Charlotte Brontë

"All women should know how to take care of children. Most of them will have a husband some day."

Franklin P. Jones

"Never trust a husband too far, nor a bachelor too near."

Helen Rowland

"I know one thing about men.
[Husbands] never die when you
want them to."

Suzanne Finnamore

"Before I met my husband,
I'd never fallen in love. I'd stepped
in it a few times."

Rita Rudner

"My husband wanted to be cremated. I told him I'd scatter his ashes at Neiman Marcus. That way, I'd visit him every day."

Joan Rivers

"Wives in their husbands'
absences grow subtler,
And daughters sometimes run
off with the butler."

Lord Byron

"Behind every successful man is
a proud wife and a surprised
mother-in-law."

Hubert H. Humphrey

"Plain women are always jealous
of their husbands. Beautiful women
never are. They are always so
occupied with being jealous of other
women's husbands."

Oscar Wilde

"Think of your husband as a house. You are allowed to give him a fresh coat of paint and change out the furniture now and then. But if you're constantly trying to pour a new foundation or replace the roof, you're in serious trouble."

Peter Scott

"The faults of husbands are often caused by the excess virtues of their wives."

Sidonie Gabrielle Colette

"To catch a husband is an art;
to hold him is a job."

Simone de Beauvoir

"The man who says his wife
can't take a joke, forgets that
she took him."

Oscar Wilde

"A man's mother is his misfortune,
but his wife is his fault."

Walter Bagehot

"I don't think a prostitute is more
moral than a wife, but they are
doing the same thing."

Prince Philip

"Middleage is the time of life that a man first notices in his wife."

Richard Armour

"If you are really Master of your Fate, it shouldn't make any difference to you whether Cleopatra or the Bearded Lady is your mate."

Ogden Nash

"The calmest husbands make
the stormiest wives."

Thomas Dekker

"Five wives can't all be wrong."

J. Paul Getty